THE LITTLE BOOK OF
COFFEE

Published by OH!
20 Mortimer Street
London W1T 3JW

Text © 2021 OH!
Design © 2021 OH!

Disclaimer:

All trademarks, quotations, company names, registered names, products, characters, logos and catchphrases used or cited in this book are the property of their respective owners. This book is a publication of OH!, an imprint of Welbeck Publishing Group Limited, and has not been licensed, approved, sponsored, or endorsed by any person or entity. All rights reserved. No part of this publication may be reproduced, stored in a retrieval system, or transmitted in any form or by any means (including electronic, mechanical, photocopying, recording, or otherwise) without prior written permission from the publisher.

ISBN 978-1-80069-017-2

Compiled by: Victoria Godden, Rosie Field
Editorial: Lisa Dyer
Project manager: Russell Porter
Design: Tony Seddon
Production: Freencky Portas

A CIP catalogue record for this book is available from the British Library

Printed in Dubai

10 9 8 7 6 5 4 3 2 1

Illustrations: Freepik.com

THE LITTLE BOOK OF
COFFEE

FRESHLY GROUND WORDS
OF WIT AND WISDOM

CONTENTS

INTRODUCTION

Coffee is enjoyed all around the world by a great many people, but legend has it that we have an Ethiopian goat herder called Kaldi to thank for its discovery, all the way back in the 9th century. And, boy oh boy, it has come a long way since then!

Over 2 billion cups of coffee are drunk every day around the world, so what gives it such a global appeal? For some it's a case of receiving that all-important jolt of caffeine first thing in the morning, while for others it's all about the methodical preparation of the perfect cup, not to mention the delicious aroma and taste.

Gertrude Stein described coffee as "an event", and there's nothing like the offer of "going for a coffee" to warm the cockles of your heart. Coffee has become an essential accompaniment to our weekly meetings; coffee shops have become our destination for catching up with friends and sometimes even our meeting place for dates. As such, coffee has become so much more that simply something to rouse us into consciousness in the mornings!

If you don't feel human until you've had your first cup of joe, or you count yourself as a real coffee connoisseur, then this book is for you.

CHAPTER
ONE

Wake up and smell the coffee!

Sometimes it's the thought of that first cup of coffee that gets us out of bed in the morning.

For many of us it's hard to function until we've had our first sips of that delicious, hot, bitter liquid. So, just like that first caffeine hit of the day, let's kickstart our celebration of all things coffee!

"

If this is coffee,
please bring me
some tea; if this is
tea, please bring
me some coffee.

"

Abraham Lincoln

66

Amazing how the world begins to change through the eyes of a cup of coffee.

99

Donna A. Favors

Legend has it that coffee was discovered by an Ethopian goat herder who noticed that his goats became extremely energetic after eating certain berries.

"

Once you wake up and smell the coffee, it's hard to go back to sleep.

"

Fran Drescher

Coffee comes
from the
Coffea plant.

Coffee is a fruit.

The "beans" are actually the pit of a berry, sometimes called a coffee cherry.

66

What goes best
with a cup of coffee?
Another cup.

99

Henry Rollins

66

My birthstone is a coffee bean.

99

Anonymous

"

Love is in the
air and it smells
like coffee.

"

Unknown

There are two main
types of coffee:

Arabica

and

Robusta.

Arabica coffee was originally cultivated on the Arabian Peninsula, hence the name. **Robusta** coffee is a more hardy plant and has twice the amount of caffeine.

Arabica is descended from the original coffee trees discovered in Ethiopia, and these produce a fine, mild, aromatic coffee and represent approximately **70%** of the world's coffee production. The beans are flatter and more elongated than **robusta** and lower in caffeine.

Robusta coffee is used in blends and for instant coffees.

These beans tend to be slightly rounder and smaller than **arabica** beans.

Coffee grows best
in rich soil, with
mild temperatures,
frequent rain and
shaded from the sun.

66
I never laugh until I've had my coffee.
99

Clark Gable

Although yields
vary with each harvest,
in a year,

a single coffee bush

only usually provides
enough coffee beans to fill

a half-kilo bag

of ground coffee.

"

Among the numerous luxuries of the table... coffee may be considered as one of the most valuable. It excites cheerfulness without intoxication; and the pleasing flow of spirits which it occasions... is never followed by sadness, languor or debility.

"

Benjamin Franklin

Coffee is the world's second-largest traded commodity after crude oil.

66

I like coffee
because it gives
me the illusion that
I might be awake.

99

Lewis Black

All commercially grown
coffee is from a region of
the world called
the Coffee Belt.

66

May your coffee kick in before reality does.

99

Anonymous

"

Without my
morning coffee, I'm
just like a dried-up
piece of roast goat.

"

Johann Sebastian Bach

Cafephile

is the word for
a coffee
lover.

66

I think if I were a
woman, I'd wear
coffee as a perfume.

99

John Van Druten

Top 10
Coffee-Producing Countries

1. Brazil
2. Vietnam
3. Columbia
4. Indonesia
5. Ethiopia
6. Honduras
7. India
8. Uganda
9. Mexico
10. Peru

"

Life is too short for bad coffee.

"

Unknown

"

Mornings are for coffee and contemplation.

"

Jim Hopper

> **Procaffeination (n):**
> the tendency to
> not start anything until
> you've had
> a cup of coffee.

Unknown

"

The best maxim
I know in this life is to
drink your coffee
when you can, and
when you cannot, to be
easy without it.

"

Jonathan Swift

66

The smell of
fresh-made coffee
is one of the world's
greatest inventions.

99

Hugh Jackman

"

We want to do a lot of stuff, we're not in great shape. We didn't get a good night's sleep. We're a little depressed. Coffee solves all these problems in one delightful cup.

"

Jerry Seinfeld

Good communication
is just as stimulating as
black coffee, and just
as hard to sleep after.

Anne Morrow Lindbergh

CHAPTER
TWO

Where have you bean?

Coffee is drunk all around the world, with many different countries enjoying their own ways of preparing and serving it.

So, if your idea of a speciality coffee is a caramel latte, read on and discover that that's just the tip of the iceberg!

The world's first
coffee house
opened in

1475

in Constantinople
(modern-day
Istanbul).

Kaisermelange

is a type of Austrian coffee drink. Egg yolk is mixed with honey and then hot black coffee is added in slowly - delicious!

In parts of Scandinavia, coffee is served with cheese!

Called *kaffeost*, cubes of cheese are added to coffee, creating a delicious drink said to taste a bit like tiramisu.

Nous nous
is a Moroccan
coffee meaning
"half half". A strong
shot of coffee is
topped with half
a glass of heated,
frothy milk.

The word

coffee

comes from
the Arabic word

qahwah

which
means "wine".

In Greece, you will find various **_kafenio_**, which are old-fashioned coffee shops. Extremely popular with older gentlemen, they are a favourite meeting place to drink coffee, talk politics and play cards.

The Turks
call their
coffee houses
"schools
for the wise".

Hawaii

is the only
American state
that grows coffee.

66

I make a mean
cup of coffee, if
you give me the
right ingredients.

99

Ice Cube

In Portugal there's
a hot coffee drink
called *galão*. Closely
related to the latte and
cappuccino, it contains
about twice as much
foamed milk, making it
a lighter drink.

Top 10

Coffee-Drinking Countries in the World

1. Finland
2. Norway
3. Iceland
4. Denmark
5. The Netherlands
6. Sweden
7. Switzerland
8. Belgium
9. Luxembourg
10. Canada

The Dutch East India Company

brought coffee seedlings to Batavia (present-day Jakarta), their former capital city on the island of Java in 1696. By 1706 the first sample of Java coffee was sent to Amsterdam for sampling along with one coffee plant. In the 19th and early 20th century, coffee from Java grew more and more popular, and Java became synonymous with coffee.

Kopi lumak from Indonesia is the most expensive coffee in the world.
It's made from beans digested from the Asian palm civet (a small cat). It sells for

350 euros

per kilo!

The Coffee Belt,
where the ideal coffee-
growing conditions
are found, is located
between latitudes
25 degrees north
and
30 degrees south.

Europe

imports more
coffee than the

USA

66

Coffee is a
language in itself.

99

Jackie Chan

Brazil

produces the most
coffee in the world,
followed by

Vietnam.

Finland

consumes the most coffee in the world!

The Ivory Coast

is one of the world's largest producers of **robusta** coffee.

Irish coffee

is extremely popular worldwide. It seems like the blend of hot coffee, whisky and cream is too good to resist.

Café de olla is a traditional Mexican coffee beverage, prepared using a traditional earthen clay pot and flavoured with cinnamon, sugar and sometimes orange peel, anise and cloves.

Kopi joss is a specialty coffee enjoyed in Indonesia. What makes this coffee unique is the addition of **burning charcoal**, added directly into the cup of coffee. It's said to have health benefits.

The traditional vessel for boiling Turkish coffee is called an *ibrik*.

Turkish coffee is made with cold water, ground **arabica** coffee, sugar and cardamom, which gives it its distinctive flavour.

Einspänner is an Austrian coffee, made up of single or double espresso, topped with whipped cream.

The name comes from the German word for a single-horse carriage, which can be driven with only one hand, leaving the other free for coffee consumption.

Ethiopia

is Africa's top
producer of coffee.

In Vietnam,
coffee is enjoyed with
condensed milk.

Another popular coffee
is called *cà phê trúng*,
and is similar to a
cappuccino, except
with the addition of
an egg or two.

Make a delicious affogato at home!

Pour a shot of espresso over a scoop of your favourite vanilla ice cream for a simple and delicious dessert.

CHAPTER
THREE

A cup of joe

Whether your go-to coffee order
is an extra-hot decaf soy
vanilla latte or a simple espresso,
everyone has their favourite way
to enjoy their cup of joe.

The expression "cup of joe" is a popular nickname for a cup of coffee in America. The phrase was coined by sailors in the US Navy during World War I. A man called **Josephus Daniels** was Secretary to the Navy under President Woodrow Wilson, and Daniels imposed strict moral standards, including banning alcohol.

As a result, stewards bought more drinks such as coffee, and the phrase "a cup of Joseph Daniels" was born, later shortened to "cup of Joe".

"

Coffee was only
a way of stealing
time that should
by rights belong
to your slightly
older self.

"

Terry Pratchett

The trick to
a tasty cup of coffee
is using
filtered
water.

66

Even bad coffee
is better than no
coffee at all.

99

David Lynch

Louis XV of France

grew his own coffee beans in greenhouses at Versailles, handpicked them, roasted and ground them and served his homemade brew to guests.

35%

of coffee drinkers
take it black.

"

I like my coffee
like I like myself:
strong, sweet and
too hot for you.

"

Jac Vanek

Keep your coffee fresh

Always store opened coffee beans in an airtight container. Glass canning jars or ceramic storage crocks with rubber-gasket seals are good choices.

"

I would rather suffer with coffee than be senseless.

"

Napoleon Bonaparte

American President Theodore Roosevelt drank a **gallon** of coffee **every day**.

"

Never trust anyone who doesn't drink coffee.

"

A. J. Lee

Ground coffee and single-serve coffee pods are becoming increasingly popular, particularly among those aged 16–34, who account for **16%** of all buyers.

Coffee has been **banned** at least three times in three different cultures: once in Mecca in the 16th century; once by Charles II of England in an attempt to suppress an ongoing revolution; and once by Frederick the Great, in Germany in 1677, who was concerned people were spending too much money on the drink.

Most popular coffee orders

Americano
Caffè latte
Caffè mocha
Café au lait
Flat white
Cappuccino
Cold-brew coffee
Double espresso
Espresso
Espresso macchiato

"

Black as the
devil, hot as hell,
pure as an angel,
sweet as love.

"

**Charles Maurice de Talleyrand-Périgord,
on how he liked his coffee**

Cappuccino

got its name after the resemblance of its colour to that of the robes worn by monks of the **Capuchin order**.

A Belgian named
George Washington
invented

instant coffee

in **1906**
in Guatemala.

"

What on earth
could be more
luxurious than a
sofa, a book and a
cup of coffee.

"

Anthony Trollope

A **double espresso** is also known as a *doppio.*

"

You can't have a
decent food culture
without a decent
coffee culture: the
two things grow
up together.

"

Adam Gopnik

Different types of
coffee makers

French press or cafetière
Percolator
Single serve
AeroPress
Drip
Pour over
Cold brew
Moka

Dalgona coffee recipe

Ingredients

3 tbsp instant coffee
2 tbsp sugar
400-500ml (1¾-2 cups) milk

Method

Whisk the coffee, sugar and 3 tbsp
of boiling water in a bowl for
approximately 5 minutes until
the mixture is thick and fluffy
with stiff peaks.

For hot coffee, gently heat the milk and
pour into two heatproof glasses. For
cold coffee, pour the cold milk into two
glasses. Divide the coffee mixture in half
and spoon evenly on top of the glasses.

CHAPTER
FOUR

Espresso yourself

You can't walk down the street without seeing someone with a portable coffee cup in hand.

Having a cup of coffee is an event, and coffee culture is booming.

"

The first cup is for the guest, the second for enjoyment, the third for the sword.

"

Old Arabic saying

The "Big Four" coffee roasting companies – **Kraft**, **P&G**, **Sara Lee** and **Nestlé** – buy about **50%** of the coffee produced worldwide.

"

Our culture runs on coffee and gasoline, the first often tasting like the second.

,,

Edward Abbey

Starbucks, **Dunkin' Donuts** and **Tim Hortons** are the three largest coffee chains in the world.

Espresso

comes from the
Italian, meaning
"expressed" or
"forced out".

On the high street,
café culture has also
continued to boom.
80% of people who
visit coffee shops do so
at least once a week,
while **16%** of us visit
on a daily basis.

66

Hot coffee and cold winter mornings are two of the best soulmates who ever did find each other.

99

Terri Guillemets

80% of UK households buy instant coffee for in-home consumption, particularly those aged 65 and older.

66

Everything in my life has something to do with coffee.

99

Lorelai Gilmore, *Gilmore Girls*

In the UK,
we now drink
approximately
95 *million*
cups of coffee
per day.

Source: The British Coffee Association

In Turkey, coffee is often served with a **glass of water** so the drinker is able to cleanse their palate. A small sweet treat, like Turkish delight or chocolate candies, is often also served with the drinks.

66

Adventure in life is good; consistency in coffee even better.

99

Justina Chen

In **Finland**, coffee is often enjoyed with *korvapuusti* cinnamon buns.

In the **Middle East**, coffee is served from a special pot called a *dallah* and small, handle-less cups called *fenjan*. Guests are typically served dates or candied fruit along with their coffee.

66

It's just like when you've got some coffee that's too black, which means it's too strong. What do you? You integrate it with cream, you make it weak ... it used to wake you up, now it puts you to sleep.

99

Malcolm X

Enjoy sugar in your coffee? Danish philosopher **Søren Kierkegaard** was reported to make his coffee by filling a cup with sugar and adding black coffee to dissolve it.

66

May your coffee be strong and your Monday be short.

99

Unknown

When enjoying a cup of coffee, the four main flavour types to consider are the **acidity**, the **bitterness**, the **sweetness** and the **saltiness**.

Coffee tip!

For a delicious cup of coffee,
warm your cup under
hot water before pouring.

The level of roasting
impacts the coffee aroma.

Research has suggested
that lighter roasts
have **herby** and **fruity**
notes, while darker roasts
have **smoky** and **burnt**
aromas.

Coffee tip!

Don't use boiling water when you make your cup of joe! The perfect temperature is **90-96°C** (194-205°F).

66

Coffee, which makes
the politician wise,
and see through
all things with his
half-shut eyes.

99

Alexander Pope

It has been suggested that the best time to drink coffee is **mid to late morning**, when your cortisol levels are lower.

In the UK, people
consume on average
two cups of coffee
a day, although
there are significant
differences in this
figure among varying
age groups.

"

To an old man, a
cup of coffee is
like the door post
of an old house
– it sustains and
strengthens him.

"

Old Bourbon proverb

66

I like my coffee like
I like my women.
In a plastic cup.

99

Eddie Izzard

CHAPTER
FIVE

A latte love

Coffee is one of the chicest everyday beverages out there and has been the drink of choice for many of the world's greatest artists.

So, next time you need some inspiration, get brewing!

66

As soon as coffee is in your stomach, there is a general commotion. Ideas begin to move ... similes arise, the paper is covered. Coffee is your ally and writing ceases to be a struggle.

99

Honoré de Balzac

"
If it wasn't for
coffee, I'd have
no discernible
personality at all.
"

David Letterman

66

Coffee gives you time to think. It's a lot more than just a drink; it's something happening. Not as in hip, but like an event, a place to be, but not like a location, but like somewhere within yourself. It gives you time, but not actual hours or minutes, but a chance to be, like be yourself, and have a second cup.

"

Gertrude Stein

Author
Margaret Atwood
has her own
"bird-friendly"
coffee blend.

66

I have measured
out my life
with coffee spoons.

99

T. S. Eliot

Beethoven
was a huge coffee
fan, meticulously
counting out
60 beans
to make a cup.

Voltaire

is said to have
drunk **40-50 cups**
of coffee every day!

66

He was my cream, and I was his coffee. And when you poured us together, it was something.

99

Josephine Baker

" Humanity runs on coffee. "

Unknown

"

That's something that annoys the hell out of me – I mean if somebody says the coffee's all ready and it isn't.

"

J. D. Salinger, *Catcher in the Rye*

> **"**
>
> There are three intolerable things in life – cold coffee, lukewarm champagne and overexcited women...
>
> **"**

Orson Welles

66

It doesn't matter where you're from – or how you feel... There's always peace in a strong cup of coffee.

99

Gabriel Bá

66

All you need is love
and more coffee.

99

Unknown

"

Without coffee, nothing gets written. Period.

"

Nancy Kress

The cafe
Les Deux Magots
in Paris is renowned
for once having
famous artists and
intellectuals as regular
guests. These included
Simone de Beauvoir,
Jean-Paul Sartre and
Ernest Hemingway.

In the TV show ***Twin Peaks***, eccentric FBI agent Dale Cooper was known for his love of a "damn fine cup of coffee" and a slice of cherry pie.

Coffee and Cigarettes
is a film by Jim
Jarmusch, which looks
at our addictions to
caffeine and nicotine.

J. K. Rowling wrote some of her early Harry Potter novels in a café called The Elephant House in Edinburgh.

"

Why do they always
put mud into coffee
on board steamers?
And why does the
tea generally taste of
boiled boots?

"

William Thackeray

66

A coffee a day
keeps a grumpy away.

99

Unknown

66

It's never too late for a coffee. After all, it's always morning somewhere in the world.

99

Zooey Deschanel

J. S. Bach wrote a short, comic opera called *Schweigt stille, plaudert nicht*, also known as *Coffee Cantata*, about a young woman called Aria who loved coffee!

"

A bad day with
coffee is better
than a good day
without it.

"

Unknown

CHAPTER
SIX

Don't worry, be frappé

Our enjoyment of coffee goes way beyond its ability to quench our thirst, so here are some final facts, useful tips and amusing anecdotes to accompany you on your morning coffee break and bring a smile to your face.

66

People don't stop eating, and they don't stop drinking coffee.

99

Magic Johnson

Did you know
you can use your
**French press/
cafetière** to
froth hot milk
for your at-home
cappuccino?

5 silly coffee jokes

How did the coffee show its love?
It said, "Words cannot espresso how much you bean to me!"

Where do birds go for a cup of joe?
To the NESTcafé.

Why did the hipster burn his tongue? *Because he drank his coffee before it was cool.*

What's the opposite of coffee?
Sneezy.

What's a barista's favourite morning mantra? *Rise and grind!*

"

Coffee and love
are best when
they are hot.

"

German proverb

Depresso:
the
feeling you get
when you've run
out of coffee.

Did you know that the first ever **webcam** watched a coffee pot? The webcam was invented at the University of Cambridge in 1991 and was used to monitor how much coffee was left in the pot, in order to help people avoid pointless trips to the coffee pot if there was none left!

"

Science may never
come up with
a better office
communication
system than the
coffee break.

"

Earl Wilson

Drinking coffee
may have health
benefits, including
a reduced risk
of illnesses like
cancer, **heart
disease** and
Alzheimer's.

Coffee was originally regarded as a wonder drug in **Yemen** and **Arabia** and was taken only on the advice of a doctor.

" Coffee is the best medicine. "

Anonymous

"

The powers of a man's mind are directly proportional to the quantity of coffee he drank.

"

Sir James Mackintosh

66

I judge a restaurant
by the bread and
the coffee.

99

Burt Lancaster

"

I love having
a croissant and a
great cup of coffee.
Just one cup.

"

Marcus Samuelsson

66

When life gives you lemons, trade them for coffee.

99

Anonymous

"

No one can understand the truth until he drinks of coffee's frothy goodness.

"

Sheik Abd-al-Kadir

5 coffee puns for the coffee lover

I made a pot of coffee, espresso-ly for you.

You mocha me very happy.

I love brew. I honestly love brew.

Thanks a latte for being my friend.

Where have you bean all my life?

Tiramisu,

the Italian coffee-flavoured dessert, literally translates as "pick me up" or "cheer me up".

The term
barista
comes from
the Italian for
"bartender".

5 delicious biscuits to serve with coffee

Crunchy almond biscotti

Lotus Biscoff biscuits

All-butter shortbread

Chocolate florentines

Chocolate-chip cookies

Take your cooking up a notch by using coffee!

Enhance the richness
of your favourite brownie recipe
by adding a splash of coffee to
the mixture.

Coffee also adds a nice flavour to
a big bowl of hot chilli.

There is
95mg
of caffeine
in an average
cup of coffee.

Java
is a specific
type of **arabica**
coffee bean.

Roasting coffee

transforms the
chemical and physical
properties of green
coffee beans
into roasted coffee
products.

The roasting process
is what produces the
characteristic flavour
of coffee by causing
the green coffee beans
to change in taste,
ultimately bringing
out the different
aromas and tastes.

Decaffeinated coffee

has the caffeine removed
from the coffee beans, usually
at the green or unroasted stage,
and decaffeinated coffee
by definition has

97%

of the caffeine removed.

Grinding is done after the roasting of the beans and just before brewing the coffee. Depending how you make it, you should consider the following.

For French press:
Grind the coffee to large-size grind.

For drip brewing:
Grind to a medium-sized grind.

For espresso:
Grind to a fine-sized grind.

Starbucks' infamous *Pumpkin Spiced Latte* is now available in 50 countries worldwide.

A coffee plant
can live up to

100
years.

About
170 million
sacks of coffee
are produced in the
world every year.

International
Coffee Day is on

October
1

Espresso Martini Recipe

Ingredients

Sugar syrup

Ice

100ml (3oz) vodka

50ml (1½oz) freshly brewed espresso coffee

50ml (1½oz) coffee liqueur

4 coffee beans (optional)

Method

Pour 1 tbsp of sugar syrup into a cocktail shaker along with a handful of ice, the vodka, espresso and coffee liqueur. Shake until the outside of the cocktail shaker feels icy cold.

Strain into two chilled glasses and garnish each one with coffee beans.

The coffee industry creates over **1,700,000** jobs in the US, according to the National Coffee Association.

66

Decaffeinated coffee is kind of like kissing your sister.

99

Bob Irwin

"

I gave up coffee.
It's almost worse than
giving up a lover.

"

Sandra Bullock

66

You can tell when you've crossed the frontier into Germany because of the badness of the coffee.

99

King Edward VII

DIY coffee body scrub

Mix half a cup of freshly ground coffee with half a cup of brown sugar and half a cup of coconut oil and – voila! A scrumptious shower scrub, which will leave you ready to start the day!

66

A yawn is a silent
scream for coffee.

99

Rachel Hollis

In the old days,
cowboys were known
to brew their coffee by
putting some into a **sock**
and then putting it in
cold water and heating
it over a campfire.

Most coffee sacks
are made from
hemp.

You can use coffee
grounds to scour
your pots and pans.
Their abrasive
texture helps
scrape away
caked-on food.

66
Life happens, coffee helps.
99

Unknown